# Endorsements

In Beeline to the Cross, Joel Littlefield invites the reader on a journey into the white-hot reality of the cross-centered life. With Charles Spurgeon as an exegetical escort, this book elevates Jesus Christ as the axis around which all of Scripture must rotate. I recommend this work for pastors, teachers, students, and all those whose lives have been informed, reformed, and transformed by the life-giving power of the cross.

—Christian T. George, Ph.D.
Assistant Professor of Historical Theology
Curator of the Spurgeon Library
Midwestern Baptist Theological Seminary
Kansas City, Missouri

Beeline to the Cross is a powerful book. The message is clear, refreshing, and exactly what's needed for believers in today's dangerous world. Persecuted saints in the Middle East cling to the Cross and so should we. In all of life's ups and downs make a Beeline to the Cross.

—Tom Doyle
Middle East Director for e3 Partners and Author of Dreams and Visions—Is Jesus Awakening the Muslim World? and Killing Christians-Living the Faith Where it is NOT Safe to Believe.

"Beeline to the Cross" will ignite a passion and joy in your soul for what Jesus has done through the cross. Joel Littlefield gives us a powerful look into the work of Christ. It is enjoyable, accessible, and challenging.

—Philip Nation,
Author of "Habits for Our Holiness"
Director of Content Development LifeWay Christian Resources

"The cross of Christ is the hinge of history, not merely of human history but of cosmic history. Existence is absurd until we understand the cross. It's why Spurgeon always made "a beeline to the cross" in every sermon on every text he preached. And it's why Joel has written this very helpful book. He helps us survey the wondrous cross and see in the death of the Prince of Glory the spring of all our hope and joy."

—Jon Bloom,
Author and Co-founder, Desiring God

# BEELINE
## *to the*
# CROSS

# BEELINE
## — *to the* —
# CROSS
#### FOR SALVATION AND ALL OF LIFE

*Joel Littlefield*

WIPF & STOCK · Eugene, Oregon

Wipf and Stock Publishers
199 W 8th Ave, Suite 3
Eugene, OR 97401

Beeline to the Cross
For Salvation and All of Life
By Littlefield, Joel
Copyright © 2016 by Littlefield, Joel All rights reserved.
Softcover ISBN-13: 978-1-7252-8508-8
Hardcover ISBN-13: 978-1-7252-8510-1
eBook ISBN-13: 978-1-7252-8509-5
Publication date 7/22/2020
Previously published by Tate Publishing, 2016

*I want to express my first and deepest thanks to my Savior, Jesus Christ, to the Spirit of Comfort who dwells in me, and to my gracious Father who loves me. Apart from You I can do nothing.*

*Thank you, Callie, for your patience and support of my writing. You are the greatest helper, most gracious and beautiful companion this man could ever ask for.*

*Micah, Nathanael and Aliyah, my sweet children, I'm not sure how aware you are now of your sacrifice, but I love your understanding through the hours of my writing this book. I'm blessed to be your Daddy.*

*Thank you, Louise, for taking the time to read and edit my early drafts. Sorry for all the commas.*
*-Your Protestant friend, Joel*

*Mom, thank you for all your feedback and support through the editing process.*

*To all my family, friends and readers; thank you all so much! You have no I idea how much it blesses me to write for you!*

# Contents

Introduction ............................................................. 13
Chapter 1   Following Begins at the Cross ................. 17
Chapter 2   There Was a Barrier ................................. 21
Chapter 3   God of Joy .............................................. 27
Chapter 4   The Path of Joy ...................................... 31
Chapter 5   Fullness of Joy ........................................ 35
Chapter 6   Brokenness at the Cross ......................... 43
Chapter 7   Mercy's Appeal for Brokenness ............... 49
Chapter 8   Inward Cleansing at the Cross ................ 51
Chapter 9   A Contrite Heart .................................... 55
Chapter 10  Love Displayed at the Cross .................... 59
Chapter 11  Made Friends through the Cross ............. 65
Chapter 12  He Loved us First .................................... 69
Chapter 13  A Crushing Blow from The Cross ........... 75
Chapter 14  The Cross over Fear ................................ 79
Chapter 15  The Greatest Satisfaction ......................... 85
Chapter 16  A Full Portion ........................................ 89

# Introduction

How important is the Cross of Jesus Christ? It is so significant and so weighty that even the non-Christian gives *some* value and reverence to it. But what about you, the Christian whose desire is to live in a way that is meaningful and glorifying to God? Are you receiving every bit of what the cross was meant to do, not only for your salvation, but for your daily life?

I have one goal with this book, to bring you to the cross and to show you the value of what happened there. No matter what you are facing, the trial, the circumstance, or the joy at hand, the cross of Jesus Christ must be your ultimate aim and hope. It is there that you and I need to go, always.

Charles Spurgeon once said in regards to his method of preaching, "I take my text and *make a beeline to the cross.*" I love preaching, preachers, and reading the greats of the past, so naturally I was drawn to what he said. I was overwhelmed at the simplicity and wisdom of his statement. But I realize now that this is not a philosophy for preaching only, but for all of life. It is something that I greatly desire for my own life and for you who are reading this.

To make a beeline means "to go quickly in a straight, direct course." You might be thinking, "I've never seen a bee fly this way." Actually, neither have I, but it happens. The expression comes from the forager bee. When a bee finds a source of nectar, it flies back to the hive to perform a very peculiar dance before the other bees. In this dance he is expressing the exact coordinates of the find to the rest of the hive. The other bees leave the nest making a *beeline* to the source of nectar. They make a direct course to the very place that supplies the life to their hive. Without the nectar they have no life. Can you see where Spurgeon was coming from? He knew the source of all things. He knew that Jesus Christ was the only way to eternal life, the only hope for sinners. It was there that he directed his own eyes and the eyes of others.

Now apply this to yourself, knowing who the source of life truly is. Be honest, and ask yourself these questions. Where do you run to when things get hard, when the pain of life is nearly too much to bear? Where do you go when you need wisdom and understanding, when there seems to be no good answers for your troubles? Where do you set your eyes in the very moment that you begin to suffer, that moment when you lose someone close or when the doctor breaks the news that you're sick? What gets your attention the most when you are rewarded, when you experience joy and happiness? Who gets the praise for all that is good right now in your life, for your home, your spouse and your beautiful children? Are you daily making a *beeline to the cross, to the source of life*, to the Creator of all things? The wooden cross holds no power on its own, but the man who died there for the sin of the world and holds all the power in the universe does.

Believe me, I'm asking myself the same questions. I realize that not one human is exempt from this desperate need for Jesus at every moment. From the very beginning when the Father drew you to His Son, to the moment you draw your very last breath, you need Him like you need oxygen. You need His omnipresent embrace, His power, His perfect wisdom and comfort. You need His Word, His life, His example of love and sacrifice. The cross is a symbol of that sacrifice. The cross is your visual reminder of the price paid for salvation, a price you could never afford.

When you choose to go to the cross and when you go often, you will begin to realize that reconciliation with God is only the beginning of what He has planned for you.

1 Corinthians 2:9 "But, as it is written, 'What no eye has seen, nor ear heard, nor the heart of man imagined, what God has prepared for those who love him.'"

Imagine how much God longs to encourage you, to refresh you, to affirm you, and to sustain you. Imagine how

He will fill you with overwhelming joy through Christ. Consider how He has and will conquer all the enemies of those who believe and rest in Jesus, the greatest cross bearer. Reflect on these things and then remember that your finite mind cannot possibly visualize the extent of it all. God's plan is infinitely and abundantly bigger.

Ephesians 3:20 "Now to him who is able to do far more abundantly than all that we ask or think, according to the power at work within us, to him be glory in the church and in Christ Jesus throughout all generations, forever and ever. Amen."

I believe the cross, where Jesus shed His innocent blood for sinners, is the most pivotal place in human history. I can only hope that you will examine what I write with honest reflection upon the Word, the final authority, and that you will take heed to what He reveals to your heart.

# Chapter 1
# Following Begins at the Cross

*"All the ages meet in Calvary. Jesus is the central Sun of all events."*

—*Spurgeon*

THE LESSONS WE learn in our early days with Christ are invaluable. The beginning is most valuable of all. The foundation of our walk of faith is Christ, and He lays it with just two words, "Follow me."

These are words of power and authority, words with eternal life and absolute purpose.

What does it mean to follow Jesus?

I believe it starts with a "beeline," a direct course to Calvary, "the central Sun of all events." This is where all eternity is focused. This is where you must focus.

When Jesus called the twelve, each one had to leave something behind. Following one thing always involves a leaving of another and it's no different with your call to follow after Christ.

Whether called from their businesses or careers, their comforts, families, or future goals, the Disciples were called before they knew anything of the cross. In the days that followed, they learned that following Jesus had *everything* to do with the cross.

Matthew 16:24 "If anyone would come after me, let him deny himself, and take up his cross and follow me."

Jesus is saying, *if you want to follow me, it starts with denying self, and clinging to a cross.* This, no doubt, challenges the heart of sinful man. He wasn't speaking of His own cross here, for only He could bear that one. Instead, He was speaking of a willingness to associate with all that the cross means, both for Jesus then, and for you today. In other words, if you are not a sold out, cross-clinging follower of Jesus, then you cannot be His disciple. You cannot follow Him.

These are His words, not mine.

They are hard words because no man wants to deny what comes naturally to him. Tell the natural man or woman not to lust after the opposite sex and he or she will think it's absurd and call you crazy.

"Why in the world would I stop what I love doing, the thing that comes naturally to me?"

Ask the natural man or woman to forsake earthly riches and he or she won't easily see the point.

He might say, "Why would I deny the very thing that buys my happiness?"

If someone says, "I follow Christ" but makes no association with His cross, that person is mistaken. Salvation is through the cross, through faith in the one who was crucified. Can a sinner be saved in his own way, and without the cross? It must be Christ's way or none at all. People say they follow God, but if the first step of that walk is not with self-denial, followed by picking up a cross, then I'm sad to say, that walk is not with Jesus.

After the resurrection the disciples saw the risen body of Christ and began to understand. They realized then what it meant to take up the cross because Jesus had displayed it for them. It meant to die, to lay everything down for the glory and the will of the Father. It meant to forsake sin, to die to it, and never look back again.

Maybe you are at the beginning of your journey with Christ. If this is so, then make every effort to examine your first steps. Let it begin with a direct course to the cross. Deny self, die to your sin and make a beeline for Jesus.

Maybe your journey with Him began a long time ago. Let this be a reminder to you, then, of your first steps, as well as your next one. Did you begin with the cross when you were called? What will you do going forward? Have you remained on the path of dying to self and to this world?

Have you shifted to a life of self-comfort? Do you minimize the reality of sin? Do you still make a direct course to Jesus every day? If you have strayed from the centrality of the cross, then this is the day you must repent and return. Be sure of this; if you are His, then you are His forever, but the cross must be the central theme of your life. Make a beeline. Go now to Calvary in your mind and let the full weight of the cross affect you. Commit again today to the life of a sold-out, cross-clinging, sin-crucifying, forgiven follower of Jesus.

# Chapter 2
# There Was a Barrier

*"When sin is gone, the barrier is broken down, the unfathomable gulf is filled. Pardon, which removes sin, and justification, which brings righteousness, make up a deed of clearance so real and so complete that nothing now divides the sinner from his reconciled God."*

—*Spurgeon*

SOMETHING TOOK PLACE on Calvary that allows men not only to *become* followers, but to *continue* faithfully. Again, our focus is the cross, the event that crowns all of human history. Make a direct course for the cross to find out how the very things that are impossible with man, become possible with God.

The sacrificial death of Jesus removed the barrier that stood between man and God. When Adam and Eve sinned, a veil was formed, and brought total separation. The veil was not a visible one until the first tabernacle, but the weight of its separating power was felt by all mankind. The liberty in which Adam once walked, and his absolute open policy to talk and walk with God were now impossible. Man's love for self over God got him cast out of his Maker's presence.

Once the veil was visible, it would be a statement to the entire world that God is holy and that getting to Him is not by a mere act of the human will and desire, but by an act of God's will. Only through His prescribed way.

For this, a system was implemented for His people. A chosen priest, an altar, and a spotless lamb sacrificed for a sinful race in need. Once per year the high priest carefully entered with a specific offering. The blood of the slain substitute was placed on the mercy seat to atone for the sins of Israel. Through this lens, the lens of innocent blood, God chose to see His people. Israel's sins could be covered, but only by the blood of that sacrifice.

You could say that all eyes were on that altar, on that mercy seat. God was showing the way to reconciliation, a holy God acting in mercy to cover sin, because He loves to glorify His name.

Romans 9:16 "So then it depends not on human will or exertion, but on God, who has mercy."

All of this was a shadow of better things to come. It all foreshadowed Jesus Christ our High Priest and spotless Lamb. The altar represented the cross where His blood was spilled. On the third day, He rose from the grave in victory over death, and would ascend to Heaven, the true mercy seat of God. As the only worthy High Priest, Jesus entered bearing the scars of His death on His body. The Father approved, and Jesus remains in glory, seated at the right hand of the throne to ever intercede for us.

Hebrews 10:19-20 "Therefore, brothers, since we have confidence to enter the holy places by the blood of Jesus, by the new and living way that he opened for us through the curtain, that is, through His flesh, and since we have a great priest over the house of God, let us draw near with a true heart in full assurance of faith"

Consider your life. If you are following Jesus, then you are in fact doing the impossible right now. No man can follow God unless *God* makes the way. No man is innocent unless Christ's innocence is placed upon Him. As a believer you are walking and communing with a holy, righteous God who has every right to punish you for sin. Instead, He has brought you through the veil of separation to behold His mercy, and receive His riches.

Isaiah 25:7-8 "And he will swallow up on this mountain the covering that is cast over all peoples, the veil that is spread over all nations. He will swallow up death forever; and the Lord GOD will wipe away tears from all faces, and the reproach of His people He will take away from all the earth, for the LORD has spoken."

In the Old Testament, the place of God's mercy was symbolized in a golden artifact, the ark of God's covenant with His people. This ark was a reminder of failures, complaints, and shortcomings, for within the golden box were pieces of Israel's history that proved such shortcomings. It would remind them that even though it is utterly impossible to please God through works, through the blood of an innocent Lamb sin can be covered.

The Ark, and the sacrifices made there, points us to a more glorious work in Christ, a finished work. By grace this mystery is made known to you. You were in darkness and worthy only of death, but have been lighted upon by the Gospel of Jesus. The cross was His aim for your salvation. His blood flowed to cover your imperfection and failures. Just as through the blood on the mercy seat, through faith in Jesus, the Father sees you as righteous. Go there now and trust in His sufficient work of grace. Make a beeline to the cross where it all began for you, and where you too can pick up your cross and follow with confidence.

Hebrews 10:21-22 "and since we have a great priest over the house of God, let us draw near with a true heart in full assurance of faith, with our hearts sprinkled clean from an evil conscience and our bodies washed with pure water."

The torn flesh of Christ was the only means to a mended relationship with God. It is also the source for confidently following Christ today. Going to the cross by faith, and understanding the fullness of what took place there, is how we can find confidence to continue, no matter what.

Hebrews 10:32 "But recall the former days when, after you were enlightened, you endured a hard struggle with sufferings, sometimes being publicly exposed to reproach and affliction, and sometimes being partners with those so treated. For you had compassion on those in prison, and you joyfully accepted the plundering of your property, since you knew that you yourselves had a better possession and an abiding one. Therefore do not throw away your confidence, which has a great reward. For you have need of endurance, so that when you have done the will of God you may receive what is promised."

The believers described here in Hebrews were aware of a *better and abiding possession.* Their confidence and endurance was from the reality of the cross in their lives.

Hebrews 10:23 "Let us hold fast the confession of our hope without wavering, for he who promised is faithful."

Remember that access to God is granted by grace, not earned by deserving people. To be called a follower of Christ means you were purchased with innocent blood. It means a cross was taken up for you. Let me encourage you again to make a beeline there for confidence. Go there in your mind and with your whole heart. Let the weight of His grace and mercy bring you back to a place of awe and worship in light of all He has done for you. If you are weighed down with trials and sufferings or you are hard-hearted because of this world, go to the cross. Remember that Jesus suffered not only to give you access, but confidence in your possession of an eternal promise. You have eternal life!

James 1:12 "Blessed is the man who remains steadfast under trial, for when he has stood the test he will receive the crown of life, which God has promised to those who love him."

# Chapter 3
# God of Joy

*"Happy is our condition when the glory of God fills both heart and tongue! Oh, to swim in a sea of gratitude, to feel waves of praise breaking over one's joyful head, and then to dive into the ocean of adoration, and lose one's self in the ever-blessed God!"*

—*Spurgeon*

Psalm 4:6-8 "There are many who say, "Who will show us some good? Lift up the light of your face upon us, O Lord!" You have put more joy in my heart, than they have when their grain and wine abound. In peace I will both lie down and sleep; for you alone, O Lord, make me dwell in safety."

Set your eyes upon the place that joy was purchased, the cross of Christ. Joy is not something gained or attained by the adequate, but is God's alone to give. His joy is eternal, and uniquely different than the joy of this world. It's a joy He longs to impart.

To know joy you must know the God who is eternally joyful. To that end the question must be asked; how is God known? It's through faith in Christ. It's the Savior who makes this possible. The Scriptures teach that pure, God given joy can be known by seeing, believing and embracing a joyful God.

As joyful and radiant as God may be, He is also holy. In the previous chapter we learned that access to Him is through the sacrifice of Christ. Therefore, access to His joy, a joy we all need, is through the same. Do you desire this joy? Your desire is only part of it. It's ultimately the desire of God that makes His joy knowable. He desires to give His joy, to lavish upon His people all the riches of His glory and fill them with His life. So once again we come face to face with the cross. The cross makes it all possible. The cross makes a joyful and holy God approachable by sinners. Consider again all He accomplished in the cross for your joy in Him.

1 Chronicles 16:23-27 "Sing to the LORD, all the earth! Tell of his salvation from day to day. Declare his glory among the nations, his marvelous works among all the peoples! For great is the LORD, and greatly to be praised, and he is to be feared above all gods. For all the gods of the peoples are worthless idols, but the LORD made the

heavens. Splendor and majesty are before him; strength and *joy* are in his place."

This text begins with a command to sing, for those who have experienced the salvation of God to remember their inheritance among the nations. It's a call to declare God's glory and His marvelous works on the earth.

Why is the declaring of His praises and glory so important? Because if you do not lift *Him* up, if you do not declare *His* works and *His* glory then you *will* exalt something else; something false. Unlike the weak and worthless idols that leave man empty, the God of Israel, Jesus Christ, is a God of splendor and majesty, strength and joy. The text tells us that joy is "in His place." Joy is where He is. If we are to know this joy we must know the Maker of all, the giver of life and sustainer of Joy.

# Chapter 4
# The Path of Joy

*"Now, Beloved, is not Jesus Christ the sum and summit of your joy?"*

—*Spurgeon*

PSALM 16:11 "You make known to me the path of life; in your presence there is fullness of joy; at your right hand are pleasures forevermore."

David unknowingly prophesied of Christ when writing these words. We would do well to make these words our own. He says to the Lord "You make known to me the path of life." That is where it begins for all of us. It begins with a God given awareness that there is no life apart from Him. Without the Son there is no life, no joy and no lasting pleasure. Once you have this life through faith, you have a joy that cannot be stripped away because the eternal God purchased it for you on Calvary. His life given is His joy given, and available only through the work of the cross.

John 1:4 "In him was life, and the life was the light of men."

John 3:36 "Whoever believes in the Son has eternal life; whoever does not obey the Son shall not see life, but the wrath of God remains on him."

1 John 5:11 "And this is the testimony that God gave us eternal life, and this life is in his Son."

The Psalmist referred to a path which God had made known to him. The path of life is a path which God reveals. Apart from this there is no path to God; there is no life. Like Peter, when he confessed that Jesus was "the Christ, the Son of the living God," you too must make this profession. Once you have, then you must settle the matter, that it was not your own flesh and blood which birthed this holy confession, but your Father in Heaven who made it known.

What should you do with this God given awareness? Seek Christ with it and for more of it. See that Jesus is the Christ? Believe and follow Him every day. Confess and follow from this day forward. Maybe you will do this for the very first time upon reading this book. Then let me say on the authority of the Word of God that your sins are forgiven. Your spirit is alive, evidenced by the profession that Jesus is the Christ and worthy to be followed. You have been born again, a birth which has enabled you to see the Kingdom of God.

Some of you trusted Christ long ago and know with certainty that He is the "way, the truth, and the life." Even with that knowledge though, you still fade into discouragement at times, taking your eyes off of Jesus. The very joy that the cross was intended to bring, a joy that surpasses the ebb and flow of life, somehow seems to get lost. This should never be. The revelation of the Christ who bore the cross is a revelation for eternal joy. If it's joy you have lost, then it's the cross of Christ you need once again. You cannot pay for it or earn it. You can only return by faith to the place of purchase, to the very root of joy, and find there the eternality of what He did, and what He intends for you now. Go there and see again the fullness of joy that was paid for in the Cross of Christ.

## Chapter 5
## Fullness of Joy

*"It may well be described as the fullness of joy because it is infinite. He who drinks from a cup can soon drain it dry, but he who lies down on the brink of a great river may drink as long as he likes and he will never empty it, for he has come to its fullness."*

*Spurgeon*

PSALM 16:11 "IN your presence there is fullness of Joy."

Fullness of joy means there is nothing lacking. God's joy is complete and if you desire to have this joy, unending joy, then you need to be close to Him. This closeness comes only by the cross of Christ.

1 John 1:1-4 "That which was from the beginning, which we have heard, which we have seen with our eyes, which we looked upon and have touched with our hands,

concerning the word of life—the life was made manifest, and we have seen it, and testify to it and proclaim to you the eternal life, which was with the Father and was made manifest to us—that which we have seen and heard we proclaim also to you, so that you too may have fellowship with us; and indeed our fellowship is with the Father and with his Son Jesus Christ. And we are writing these things so that our *joy* may be complete."

John the apostle was a young man when he met Jesus. He witnessed everything Jesus said and did. He was present at the crucifixion. He touched Him, saw Him and knew Him. As a result he could testify that Jesus *is* the path to completeness of Joy. The process goes like this: Life is in the Son of God. The Son of God is the only access to fellowship with the Father. In turn there is fellowship with one another. In this restored relationship with God, having your sins blotted out, completeness of Joy is found. To maintain this joy, we need only to focus upon its origins. Joy was purchased and dispensed to an undeserving people, and this, through the cross of Christ.

Once again, make a beeline to the cross, returning to your only source of joy as one that is found in God. Consider now what took place there, how Jesus ensures your hope of joy unchanging and steadies you through all circumstances.

As you look there; see the victory. See the enemies of joy that were conquered in His cross, allowing you to rest in His victory forever.

What are some joy-thieves for the believer?

*Worry*

The Bible tells us to replace anxiety with prayer and with supplications directed towards God. To remain in worry and anxiety means to direct our supplications towards our own strength rather than to Christ's. It's that simple. Who are you trusting in; the God of joy who supplies all things? Or are you trusting in self? The state of worry steals joy because at the root of worry is idolatry. No one wants to admit that worry is a sin, especially when we are the ones doing the worrying. But what else can it be? Worrying steals the attention from God, the one who maintains joy, and causes all attention to be on self or circumstance, both of which can never supply your true need.

*The cross's response to worry*

When will worry no longer steal your joy? When you remember that nearly two millennia ago a man hung on a cross who is God of all. It is that man who said "Your Father knows what you need before you even ask." He said "Not one sparrow falls to the ground apart from your heavenly Father's care, and yet, you are more valuable than many sparrows." These words are not empty words, but they are the words of a loving Savior, whose death and resurrection ensures that this type of care is yours for all eternity. His cross makes His promises eternal for those who believe.

*Unbelief*

When you are faced with a trial and backed into a situation which tests your faith, it always comes as a two sided coin; belief in Christ's sure promises are on one side, and belief in *you* on the other side. Belief in Christ's promises rests on faith; a life of faith takes time and patience. To trust in self, on the other hand, is easier. It's tangible and often brings immediate results. It is not immediate results that God is chiefly after, but lives of faith and trust.

Unbelief steals joy because it takes you away from trusting the all-knowing, almighty God, and leaves you to depend on weak and fleshly, human wisdom. This has no power to carry you through your struggle. When there is unbelief, you are robbing yourself of seeing the mighty works of God on your behalf.

To further illustrate this all too common sin of unbelief, consider this familiar story:

Matthew 13:54-58 "and coming to his hometown he taught them in their synagogue, so that they were astonished, and said, 'Where did this man get this wisdom and these mighty works? Is not this the carpenter's son? Is not his mother called Mary? And are not his brothers James and Joseph and Simon and Judas? And are not all his sisters with us? Where then did this man get all these things?' And they took offense at him. But Jesus said to them, 'A prophet is not without honor except in his hometown and in his own household.' *And he did not do many mighty works there, because of their unbelief.*"

The mighty works that Jesus did in the regions surrounding Nazareth were not accomplished in Nazareth itself. Why? It was because of their unbelief. Consider this in your own life. Jesus wants to do mighty works in you, but unbelief will keep this from happening. If you continue in unbelief you will be robbed of the joy of seeing Christ at work.

*The cross's response to unbelief*

When will unbelief no longer steal your Joy? This is only possible when you focus on the cross in the moment of your doubt. If you think God can't handle your financial situation or hardship, remember that He conquered death. If the great foe, Satan, is no longer a threat to you because the cross conquered him, then do you think you can trust Him with everything else? Can you trust Him with your bills, your health, your safety, the welfare of your loved ones, your future, and your career? Do you believe that God who raised Christ from the dead is able to handle these things? Jesus killed death by death, and trampled it under His heel by the Spirit's resurrecting power over the grave. He did it for you. The cross paved the way to Heaven and makes joy possible in this life.

*Ungratefulness*

Ungratefulness may be the biggest threat to joy, especially in regions of great wealth. If we don't get what we want, if things do not go our way; we tend to whine, moan, kick and scream. Maybe not out loud, but it's done nonetheless, and it's hideous. Ungratefulness steals joy because it feeds self-seeking pride. Instead of being thankful in everything, knowing that God is the supplier of every good thing, you turn from Christ to self, believing you deserve or need more. Ungratefulness is doubly destructive and like a disease, not only steals your own joy, but spreads to steal the joy of those around you.

*The cross's response to ungratefulness*

When will ungratefulness no longer steal our joy? It is often said that ungratefulness comes when we do not count the blessings right in front of our faces. Even those who do not know Christ have much to be thankful for. Good gifts such as strength, family, a home, and a job are all gifts that come from God. Not everyone will glorify Him for these, but they are most definitely from Him. Beyond these material things that fade in and out of everyone's lives are gifts that belong specifically to the child of God. These are eternal gifts reserved in the Heavens and ensured by the Spirit who indwells us. The greatest gift of all is not eternal life, but Jesus, the One who *is* life and who alone gives it. To conquer ungratefulness we must remain in that place, seeing the cross, seeing Jesus who paid for all the wrong, all the evil, all the unthankfulness with His blood. He did this so that we could become the adopted of God. He did it so that we might share in His inheritance and be filled with the joy of salvation.

The cross is the place of sacrifice and substitutionary atonement. This means that in your place He died. In my place He suffered. Instead of *you* having to bear the weight of God's righteous wrath and judgment against sin, He bore it all *for* you. One of the most impactful truths of the cross is that the Father was pleased to crush His Son for sin, instead of you. That is the alternative you know. Fall on the Rock and be broken, or have the Rock fall upon you, and grind you to powder! (Luke 20:18)

The Joy of God is given eternally to those who trust Him. The cross, the place of atonement is not only your means of joy in Heaven, but your ballast for steady hope and joy in your life now. The ballast is Jesus. Your steady hope is the cross of Christ.

Do you need to humbly admit to God that you have replaced His joy with worry, unbelief, and ungratefulness? Are these three things robbing you of your daily joy? See what the Scriptures say and believe with all your heart that joy is in Him alone. Seek His presence first in your life; for in His presence is fullness and completeness of joy. Maintain this joy by living at the foot of the cross as a constant reminder of where joy was purchased. If joy seems utterly impossible to you because of pain or heartache, I challenge you to search the riches of God and see if you can exhaust the love of Christ. You cannot and you will not. Be patient. He will restore the joy you seek if you seek it in Him.

If you remain there in your unbelief, you will never find rest. Look to the cross. Believe in your heart that the blood spilled at Calvary is the only payment for your sin. Believe that Jesus is the only true God and commit your life to following Him. In this belief you will be filled with joy forevermore.

# Chapter 6
# Brokenness at the Cross

*"This race of ours became a deicide and slew the Lord, and nailed its Saviour to a tree. But he who reads the Bible with the eye of faith, desiring to discover its hidden secrets, sees something more in the Saviour's death than Roman cruelty"*

—*Spurgeon*

THE CROSS WAS a tool designed to utterly break a man; body, soul, and spirit. In Jesus' day the Roman government had mastered the arts of torture. They prided themselves and found great entertainment in bringing down their judgments upon men.

The cross was not invented by the Romans though, but was used by many cultures throughout history going as far back as the 6th century BC. In each culture, the cross was used ultimately to achieve the same outcome, death; humiliating, drawn out, excruciatingly painful death. Then why a cross for Jesus? Why was this form of death chosen for the Lord of glory?

Galatians 3:13 "Christ redeemed us from the curse of the law by becoming a curse for us—for it is written, 'Cursed is everyone who is hanged on a tree.'"

It was the plan of God for all eternity to sacrifice His beloved Son in this manner. In Psalm 22 we read words of such a graphic nature that the fact cannot be denied. The cross was always the plan, not an afterthought.

Psalm 22: 14-18 "I am poured out like water, and all my bones are out of joint; my heart is like wax; it is melted within my breast; my strength is dried up like a potsherd, and my tongue sticks to my jaws; you lay me in the dust of death. For dogs encompass me; a company of evildoers encircles me; they have pierced my hands and feet—I can count all my bones— they stare and gloat over me; they divide my garments among them, and for my clothing they cast lots."

There's a difference between the crucifixion of Christ and every other crucifixion in history. Calvary's cross took on greater meaning because the man who hung there was totally innocent. As God in human flesh, He could be nothing less. Some may ask, "Haven't other innocent men died upon a cross?" I'm sure there are many who have walked death row having never committed the crime they were accused of. Innocent men are declared guilty every day in our imperfect human courts. But not so in God's court. No matter the innocence of a man for his particular charge, guilt is something they were born with. Every man on earth is guilty before God because of the wrong committed in Eden. The curse of Adam, spiritual death, is placed on the account of the whole human race. Only Jesus, who was conceived by the Holy Spirit and born of a virgin, was without this corruption. He was the only innocent man to ever walk the earth.

As for why Jesus was destined to undergo these tortures, we will look to Calvary to find the significance. Let's look there once more.

*What did the cross do?*

The cross broke Jesus down so far that it revealed beyond the shadow of a doubt that He, God of the universe, Maker of all things, had come to earth in real flesh and bones. His dying on a cross also showed us that He had real intention, real purpose, and a real mission to accomplish. He would have bowed out long before this point if it were not the case.

As fallen man we are so full of self that we would not allow our bodies to undergo such suffering. If we had the means to speak a single word and end it all, ending our suffering and the suffering of the world, we would. So why did Jesus not end it there?

Aside from what seems obvious, that He had to die in order to make payment for sin, He also chose the cross in order to teach us something for our lives. His cross is an example for us who believe in Him. His particular way of laying down His life carries significance to strengthen us daily and to keep our hearts close to His. In His death we learn one of the greatest lessons for the believer; brokenness. Only the brutality and the beauty of the cross can accomplish this.

Look at the cross of Jesus to see the crushing, the breaking, and the humiliation He endured because of sin. It's not physical brokenness that you need (necessarily), but spiritual. It's seeing that without Jesus a person is spiritually hungry and that apart from the cross and the life given there, there is no hope; no filling. In this place of brokenness wholeness can come.

Psalm 51:1-2 "Have mercy on me, O God, according to your steadfast love; according to your abundant mercy blot out my transgressions. Wash me thoroughly from my iniquity, and cleanse me from my sin!"

The broken man knows he's a sinner. He knows that the blotting out of transgressions, the washing of iniquity, and the cleansing of sin is only possible because of someone greater than himself. These things come from a holy God who is higher than all. The Psalmist pleads, "Thoroughly wash me from my iniquity," but who can do this?

Psalm 51:3-6 "For I know my transgressions, and my sin is ever before me. Against you, you only, have I sinned and done what is evil in your sight, so that you may be justified in your words and blameless in your judgment. Behold, I was brought forth in iniquity, and in sin did my mother conceive me. Behold, you delight in truth in the inward being, and you teach me wisdom in the secret heart."

We see here that the broken are aware of their sin. The broken know that his or her sins are primarily against God. When we forget this we lose touch with the severity of sin. We forget that it was the very cause of man's separation from God in the first place. Do you recognize this when it happens in your own life? This is when things that are sinful begin to look acceptable to you. Things that are unholy become every day occurrences. For this reason, the Apostle Paul makes an appeal.

# Chapter 7
# Mercy's Appeal for Brokenness

*"'Mercy' is music, and 'tender mercy' is the most exquisite form of it, especially to a broken heart. To one who is despondent and despairing, this word is life from the dead."*

—*Spurgeon*

ROMANS 12:1 "I appeal to you therefore, brothers, *by the mercies of God*, to present your bodies as a living sacrifice, holy and acceptable to God, which is your spiritual worship."

What are the "mercies" of God? What was Paul's appeal based upon when he called believers to live holy and sacrificially as an act of worship to God? The only mercy with that kind of power is the mercy found in the cross of Christ.

When you look at the cross and embrace it as God's abundant mercy for you, how then could you make light of sin? How could we not all cringe at the thought of our lives lived in any form of disobedience to Christ, even the smallest bit? It is only the cross, God's freely given mercy that can break this thinking. Only the reality of His cross will cause you to see your sin for what it is and then mend you, making you whole again. In your brokenness, He will take you close to Himself and establish you on the Rock to live a life of adoration and praise. Isn't this reasonable in light of all He has done?

The mercy of God and the cross in particular is what brings us to the place of seeing Him in His glory and seeing our own lives in light of that glory. Until we are broken as He was broken we will not sacrifice as He sacrificed or live holy as He is holy. But with His abundant mercy in view and a daily focus on the cross where sins are pardoned we can experience true brokenness. This brokenness is a reasonable sacrifice, and the worship that follows because of it will work to increase the knowledge of His glory in our lives. This is a glory that makes sinners righteous through faith, fully acceptable and pleasing in His sight. This is a mercy that deserves our attention. This is mercy's appeal, that you would be broken as He was broken so that you might glorify the Father as He glorified the Father. What will you do with this appeal?

## Chapter 8
## Inward Cleansing at the Cross

> *"He searches the hearts, and tries the reins of the children of men. And His desire, as here expressed, is not so much anything with regard to the outward act or the tongue, or to any ceremonial performances, whatever, but first of all, it has to do with the inward parts."*
>
> —*Spurgeon*

PSALM 51:5-6 "BEHOLD, I was brought forth in iniquity, and in sin did my mother conceive me. Behold, you delight in truth in the inward being, and you teach me wisdom in the secret heart."

Is there a man on earth that was not brought forth in sin? Truly there isn't and never has there been. Original sin has affected us all. You must face this truth and feel the weight of it so as to know the depths of the pit you were drawn from by Christ. Remember your inherited sin, the death that it represents, and the debt you were born with. Not to wallow in it, but so that it might work to increase your thankfulness in light of Christ's broken body, the payment for your sin.

The confession of King David in Psalm 51 is that God desires inward cleansing and deep rooted truth in your heart. He declares that God teaches wisdom to the "secret heart." It's the place in your heart that no human intellect can access. When God accesses the secret part of your heart He teaches you of your lack without Him and the fullness you can have *with* Him. He makes you aware of your need for holiness, and that "without holiness no one shall see the Lord."

Making a beeline to the cross is the only way to real brokenness and in turn, real wholeness. It's the path to genuine humility and the only way to keep you aware of your need for His daily cleansing. Like David, you need cleansing in the inner man.

Psalm 51:7-12 "Purge me with hyssop, and I shall be clean; wash me, and I shall be whiter than snow. Let me hear joy and gladness; let the bones that you have broken rejoice. Hide your face from my sins, and blot out all my iniquities. Create in me a clean heart, O God, and renew a right spirit within me. Cast me not away from your presence, and take not your Holy Spirit from me. Restore to me the joy of your salvation, and uphold me with a willing spirit."

Joy in the salvation of God comes from the Spirit of God who dwells in your heart, a heart made clean through the righteousness of Christ. But there is a cleansing you must long for still. When you see the price paid for sin and God's mercy for sinners you'll begin to understand the seriousness of cleansing and the hideousness of sin in God's sight. Have you ever said, like David, "God, look away from my sin," knowing that sin and darkness are simply not welcome in His presence? Have you ever asked God to create in you a clean heart and a renewed spirit because you are desperate for His presence? When you speak to God in this way, and you do so based on a righteousness that is imputed to you in Christ, He will cleanse you afresh and bring joy to your soul.

What is the significance of the hyssop in Psalm 51? In the Exodus, hyssop was used by the Jews to apply the blood of the Passover lamb to the doorposts of their dwellings. Only when they did this were they passed over by God's righteous judgment. The hyssop and the blood together at Passover was a foreshadowing of Christ, our Passover, who cleanses our sin and washes our lives. In the Gospel of John we see the hyssop again. While Jesus hung on the cross He was offered a drink of bitter vinegar on a sponge. It was brought to His mouth on the end of a hyssop reed. There, the blood and the hyssop are seen together again. The blood, a covering and cleansing for sin; the hyssop, a reminder of the bitterness of sin and the brokenness

Jesus experienced. Make a beeline to the cross and see the bitterness of your own sin and how for the joy that was set before Him, Jesus endured the cross. He endured the bitterness and the brokenness so that you could be cleansed in your inner most being.

## Chapter 9
## A Contrite Heart

*"When God has put sweetness into our hearts, it is then that breaking develops the sweetness."*

—*Spurgeon*

PSALM 51:13-17 "THEN I will teach transgressors your ways, and sinners will return to you. Deliver me from bloodguiltiness, O God, O God of my salvation and my tongue will sing aloud of your righteousness. O Lord, open my lips, and my mouth will declare your praise. For you will not delight in sacrifice, or I would give it, you will not be pleased with a burnt offering. The sacrifices of God are a broken spirit; a broken and contrite heart, O God, you will not despise."

When this is your life, when you dwell in the presence of God in humility you will see great things happen. In addition to being a recipient of His grace, you will be an ambassador and teacher of His grace.

The text says "And sinners will return to you." To bring sinners to the Savior is our goal as Christians. Can this be done well in a life that is not broken? Can this be done in a life that is careless concerning holiness or in a life that disregards the severity of sin's leaven?

We also see that when we are cleared of guiltiness, and forgiven by God, the proper response is "singing aloud of His righteousness." David used the word "bloodguiltiness" and asked God to deliver him from its grasp. You may not be guilty of actual murder or the shedding of another's blood, but until we come to know the forgiveness of Jesus, we are all guilty of *His* blood. For whose sins did He take the punishment of the cross? It was yours and mine. Now you are free from guilt, if you've repented of your sins and turned to faith in Him. Now you are friends with God and set free to praise Him as you were created to do.

"The sacrifices of God are a broken spirit; a broken and contrite heart, O God, you will not despise."

Christ was utterly broken for you on the cross. He was crushed under the weight and guilt of your sin. When you look at that act of His all-out grace and mercy, are you broken by it? Are you thankful? The concluding thought of all this should be sheer amazement at this Holy God who loves sinners. The passion of God for saving sinners is a passion that breaks the true disciple, because every disciple knows he stands by the merits of Christ alone. You were once lost, but now you are found. You stand on grace alone.

Acting on this knowledge is living a life of contrition. To be contrite means "to be affected by guilt." How can a forgiven saint live in guilt if he is already forgiven? You do this by looking to the guilt of another. Look to the willingness of Jesus to become guilty in your place.

This is where you must turn once again to the cross. Christ took your guilt there: all of it. In trade, He gives you His innocence. He did it with joy in His heart. He did it for your sake and for the glory of His Father. When you make a beeline to the cross, knowing the cleansing you need, the cleansing you do not deserve, you will find a Savior who is broken. Now you can come with boldness, and you can call others to come to taste of His grace. You can open your lips and freely declare His praises with a contrite heart, one that is forgiven and loved by Christ. You can live with confidence knowing He will never despise you.

2 Corinthians 5:21 "For our sake he made him to be sin who knew no sin, so that in him we might become the righteousness of God."

# Chapter 10
# Love Displayed at the Cross

*"We are sure he loves who dies for love."*

—*Spurgeon*

JOHN 15:12-13 "THIS is my commandment, that you love one another as I have loved you. Greater love has no one than this that someone lay down his life for his friends. You are my friends if you do what I command you."

The command comes with a prior condition. Love one another *as I have loved you*. In other words, know the love of Christ, and then imitate Him amongst yourselves. Another way to say this is; the one who has been loved *by* Christ will love *like* Christ. There is no other way to love. He is the Definer, the Creator, and the example of love in its truest sense. If your definition of love does not find its flow from Him, then you do not know love at all. Instead, you have believed some cheap trick of the devil designed to counterfeit God and deceive distant hearts into thinking that love is self-defined. Some even claim "spirituality" simply based on their love for something. You may love the earth, cats, music and even show the purest of love for your spouse, but if it's not rooted in the love of Christ, then it's less than God's highest for you.

To paraphrase Paul, *without love, everything you do and say is like an obnoxious cymbal crashed in the ears of the hearer.* The Scriptures teach that not only are you to love, but to love *like* Christ. If you do not have that, then you do not know Christ like you should, and the end will be far worse than a ringing cymbal in the ear. It will be a burning hell, an eternal existence that is totally separated from the light and love of God.

What does this love look like? How can you know the love of Christ so that you might emulate it to others? Once again, going to the cross of Christ you will find all you need.

"Greater love has no one than this that someone lay down his life for his friends."

Let me say emphatically that God is the greatest! This is no opinion of mine, like stating what sort of food or sport I believe to be the greatest. The "greatness" of a created thing is determined only by the opinion of other creatures (humans), and their ability to consistently produce that level of "greatness"; not so with God. There is nothing higher, nothing more perfect, nothing like the Most High God.

2 Chronicles 2:6 "But who is able to build him a house, since heaven, even highest heaven, cannot contain him? Who am I to build a house for him, except as a place to make offerings before him?"

Love is not a created thing, but has always existed within the triune, eternal God. For this reason, love is defined in Him and by Him alone. Within the Godhead (Father, Son and Spirit), there is perfect love and unity. When God created man in His own image He created him with a capacity to love, and gave an example to follow. Without His example, man in his own fallen nature can only display glimpses of godliness in acts of love. Until a man knows the One who *is* Love, every attempt is marred with sin. We must be led to true love, taught and drawn to something that is greater than we are; someone with a real capacity and power to love. We must look to the source.

The source of love came down in human flesh, in a man named Jesus Christ. As a disciple of Christ you need to look to Him as your example to love the Church, to lay your life down as He did, and win the lost world with the gospel.

The example of true gospel-love was given very early in the Scriptures. In fact, the very first place that we find the word love in the Bible, Genesis 22, is also a very specific foreshadowing of the cross. You'll remember the story well. God had chosen a nation to be His own. This nation would be different from all the rest. The most spectacular difference would not be the laws, the rules, or the ordinances given to the Jews, but the fact that the Messiah would be born through them. Abraham and Sarah, the patriarch and matriarch of the Hebrew people, were promised a son in their old age. God said that through their line would rein a King whose throne would last forever.

Finally, after much trial and many failures, Abraham and Sarah had a son named Isaac. At first, Abraham had taken matters into his own hands, attempting to "help" God fulfill His promise with the assistance of human effort, but it failed. Amazingly, Abraham was not cast off, but instead, God proved that even his folly was part of the sovereign plan. The son of the flesh, Ishmael, and the son of promise, Isaac, would work to differentiate between the spiritual children of the flesh, and the spiritual children of promise.

So the day came when out of the blue, as I'm sure it seemed to Abraham, God commanded him to sacrifice his only son on an altar at the top of Mt. Moriah. He obeyed without hesitation.

Genesis 22:2 "Take your son, your only son Isaac, whom you *love*, and go to the land of Moriah, and offer him there as a burnt offering on one of the mountains of which I shall tell you."

This is where I want you to see Jesus. This is where you must make a beeline once more to the cross, a cross even foretold in the Old Testament. It is not by mere happenstance that the very first mention of love is found in the midst of such a selfless, God-honoring, obedient display of sacrifice. You will notice in reading the full account that Isaac was by now a grown man with the ability to carry the wood for the sacrifice upon his own shoulders. You will see that he shows no resistance to the will of his father. We know from this story that Abraham loved Isaac dearly, but loved and trusted God more. This story proves the intensity of love he had for God, enough that he would do whatever He commanded.

God's intention was never to kill Isaac, but to prove Abraham's love and faith in Him, as well as Isaac's willingness to become a sacrifice. If Isaac died before bearing his own children, it would have ended the lineage of Christ, the promised seed of Genesis chapter 3. That would never happen.

"I will put enmity between you and the woman, and between your offspring and her offspring; he shall bruise your head, and you shall bruise his heel."

God's intention from eternity was to send His only Son, a sinless sacrifice to crush death, and reign as King over all Kings, and God over all gods. The story of Moriah served not only as a picture of true love, trust, and obedience, but as a perfect foreshadowing of the greatest act of love the world would ever know.

Knowing what we know of God and seeing what we see displayed in the Scriptures, I can say with confidence that God's display of love is supreme. The laying down of an innocent life on behalf of guilty sinners, and the willingness of the Father to give His only Son in order to make us His friends forever. There is truly nothing greater. This is your example for how you, too, should love.

# Chapter 11
# Made Friends through the Cross

> *"What the invidious Jews said in bitter spleen, has been turned by the Holy Spirit to the most gracious account. Where they poured out vials of hate, odours of sacred incense arise. Troubled consciences have found a sweet balm in the very sound. Jesus, "the friend of publicans and sinners," has proved himself friendly to them, and they have become friends with him; so completely has he justified the very name which his enemies gave him in ribald affront."*
>
> *—Spurgeon*

JOHN 15:14-15 "You are my friends if you do what I command you. No longer do I call you servants, for the servant does not know what his master is doing; but I have called you friends, for all that I have heard from my Father I have made known to you."

The very nature of Christ displayed a perfect, impartial love for sinners. It is quite an amazing thing that even though sin is nowhere found in God, God in human flesh dwelt among the most vile in order to make the unclean clean. To be a friend of the world is to be at enmity with God. So who is a friend of the world? It is all who are outside of Christ. You do not have to embrace the world fully in order to be friends with it. All you must do is be distant from Christ, having never placed your faith in His name. By this alone you show your allegiance to the world.

The "friend of sinners" came to the lost and dying world on a rescue mission. He came to rescue out of this world the friends of the world, and win them through the blood of His cross. So the faith you have in Him now is evidence that He came for you. He knew you before you were born and while you were still His enemy He died for you. He loved you so dearly before you ever loved Him in return, but now that has changed. Now you *can* love Him back; and you *must*. Being His disciple, and being made one with Him by the blood of His cross, you can look back to the cross and see His friendship. Don't you desire to return this love? You are a friend of God as Abraham was. You can know this by answering one simple question; a question that takes us back to Mt. Moriah again. Are you willing to do whatever He commands; to lay down your life; to give up your rights? He is for you. Are you for Him, no matter what?

A person that does everything he's told by his master, but never really comes to know his master's heart, never fellowships and never enters his home is a good slave at best, but not a friend. A Christian, though, is both a slave of righteousness and a friend of the Righteous One, the Master, Jesus Christ. We are made friends through His cross, but we learn how to be friends with Him by looking to Him and His cross continually. Being a true friend with one another as Christians comes by taking our cues from Jesus; and more specifically, the love He displayed at the cross. He showed the Disciples His heart, His likes, His dislikes, His passions, and His sorrows. They knew Him, saw Him, touched Him, and had fellowship with Him. After all of this, after three years of life together with Jesus, He died. In His death He was saying, *my friends, this is my proof that I love you like no other can*. And so it is with us who believe today. We are His friends if we do what He says and die as He died. We have His Word. He opens the eyes of our understanding to see His commands and gives us a new heart to obey them with joy.

Everything He heard from the Father while on earth has been made known to us, and there are deep implications for embracing this truth today. This means that as a friend of Christ you have access to the heart, mind, and the will of the Father. Like Abraham, when you believe the promise of God by faith, He reveals to you the deepest, most profound act of love in the universe; the giving of His only Son for the sins of His people; for you.

## Chapter 12
## He Loved us First

> *"To me, it is one of the sweetest and most blessed truths in the whole of Revelation; and those who are afraid of it are so because they do not understand it. If they could but know that the Lord had chosen them, it would make their hearts to dance for joy."*
>
> —*Spurgeon*

How do we differentiate Christ-like love with all others? The greatest difference of all is seen when we understand the vast distance between the natural man and God because of sin.

Colossians 2:13 "And you, who were dead in your trespasses and the uncircumcision of your flesh, God made alive together with him, having forgiven us all our trespasses"

Until the Spirit brings life it is impossible for man to commune and walk with God. Prior to this, he is utterly dead and totally depraved. Find a man who has been dead for years, buried in his grave, and rotting, then expect that he might wake up to walk and run about. This is the likelihood of a man being saved by his own work and strength.

Look and see that God in His grace has acted and made the impossible to be possible.

John 15:16 "You did not choose me, but I chose you and appointed you that you should go and bear fruit and that your fruit should abide"

It is an utter shame that the doctrine of election can cause such controversy in Christian circles. I am personally disgusted that this of all subjects has divided so many friendships and fellowships over centuries. Let me be clear; the disgust lies not with the doctrine itself, or the men who have attempted to teach it or the hard Scriptures that have seemed to divide many. My disgust is with the lack of embrace and earnestness to know this important, God-exalting truth. Like all Biblical truths put forth in the Scriptures, it is our duty not to bend the truth, but to bend our understanding, so that we, the fallible creatures would come to harmonize with the infallible Word of God.

The text of John 15 says that God chooses. To deal with this text, we will not seek to alter it or find a way to fit man's wisdom into the equation in order to make it more palatable. Instead, we will accept it. God chooses

His followers. When does He choose? That's not even told in this particular passage, though it is elsewhere. But it is said very plainly here, "you did not choose me." What is he talking about? We didn't choose Him? In this context the choosing was for a very specific purpose.

"that you should go and bear fruit and that your fruit should abide, so that whatever you ask the Father in my name, he may give it to you."

The choosing mentioned here is what determines who comes to bear abiding fruit in the Vine. Not just sporadic-from time to time-when we feel like it-eventually rotting fruit, but everlasting fruit that comes from real connection to the Vine. The kind of connection where we speak to the Father in the name of Jesus, and whatever we ask, He will give it.

But there is a choosing on your part as well. It's important to ask though, "Why did you choose Him?" The question will force you to see an important truth. You will most likely answer with something similar to, "He is the only way" or "He is the only one who died for sin and rose to conquer death" or "He loved me enough to send His Son to die for me." You might say, "I love Him because without Him I'd fall apart." These are all good answers, but there is one thing that all of these answers have in common. They are responses. They are answers. They spring forth from an initiating work of God. Whether it was a broken situation, or a deep thirst, or an emptiness you felt inside, when you finally came to call on Him, you were answering a preexisting call that took place before time began.

The reason for going down this road to briefly discuss the doctrine of election is that our aim is not just to love God, but to love *who* God is, and what He has done in the Gospel. We want the highest love, the greatest example of love ever given. If this is the case, then it is not to our choosing that we should look, but to His choosing; to His love. To know the greatest love, we must look to the Lamb who was slaughtered before the worlds were made. Make a beeline to the cross. See it there in eternity, and in this, see true love.

Ephesians 1:3-5 "Blessed be the God and Father of our Lord Jesus Christ, who has blessed us in Christ with every spiritual blessing in the heavenly places, even as he chose us in him before the foundation of the world, that we should be holy and blameless before him. In love he predestined us for adoption as sons through Jesus Christ, according to the purpose of his will"

Ephesians 1:7-10 "In him we have redemption through his blood, the forgiveness of our trespasses, according to the riches of his grace, which he lavished upon us, in all wisdom and insight making known to us the mystery of his will, according to his purpose, which he set forth in Christ as a plan for the fullness of time, to unite all things in him, things in heaven and things on earth."

Go to the cross and take an inventory. What do you see there?

You see redemption through His blood, forgiveness, and the riches of grace lavished upon us by a God who is full of wisdom. See that the setting forth of Christ to die on the cross was a fulfillment of an eternal plan, one that was designed to pay the ransom for His people.

Look intently at Jesus. If you love Him, it is because He first loved you. Examine your life and all that you know about the natural man, your nature before Jesus changed you, and ask, "How did I get here?" It was His love. "How did I find Him?" He found you while you were blind. "What did I have to offer Him?" Nothing. He freely gives life, with no condition as to what man can offer Him. This is the beauty of grace. This is the gospel of free grace.

What can be said of the all too famous question, "What if I'm not chosen?" To this I would say, choose Him! Trust Him! Is your heart inclined to know Him, and to seek after Him for life? Then seize the opportunity that the Spirit has made ready for you. Believe in the only begotten Son from the Father.

As you seek to love others and win more to Christ, place your confidence in the power of God's will, God's plan to save, and God's love for the world. Place more confidence there than you do in any man's will, or power, or ability to love. With this confidence, rest assured in your salvation and in the salvation of many more to come.

## Chapter 13
## A Crushing Blow from The Cross

*"I came, I saw, I conquered," is a line which will be quoted to the end of time. Such is the life of our Lord Jesus, from the cross onward."*

—*Spurgeon*

BECAUSE OF THE cross, the spiritual warfare we engage in, our fighting, our labors, and our warring against the Enemy will not be in vain.

First, let me make clear that Jesus did not come ultimately to win wars, as in the fleshly, human, nation-against-nation kind of wars. That was not His mission. He came to win the war on sin. It's a war between the "sons of man" and the enemies of Christ, the devils who rule in spiritual realms. The war he came to fight was a sure win, a victory promised long ago, a victory that would be had through the death of an innocent sacrifice. This is why the crushing of Christ was necessary.

Matthew 26:52-54 "Then Jesus said to him, 'Put your sword back into its place. For all who take the sword will perish by the sword. Do you think that I cannot appeal to my Father, and he will at once send me more than twelve legions of angels? But how then should the Scriptures be fulfilled, that it must be so?'"

Peter's choice of what was worth physically fighting for was wrong, and vain. In fact, Jesus's statement that He could have annihilated the whole company of soldiers with a single call to the Father, but chose not to, tells us something. He could have had a legion of Angels at His side in a single moment, but he didn't. Have you seen what even one Angel of God can do, let alone a legion of them?

Isaiah 37:36 "And the angel of the Lord went out and struck down 185,000 in the camp of the Assyrians. And when people arose early in the morning, behold, these were all dead bodies."

Jesus said "But how should the scriptures be fulfilled?" In other words, if He didn't let these men bring Him harm, beat Him, rip out His beard, nail Him to a cross and kill Him, then the one crushing blow to win the battle on sin and death would never have come. What was that crushing blow? It was His death. Why the cross? Why not a complete disposal of evil at just one word? That wouldn't have dealt with the core issue, the very thing that causes evil men to act evil. The issue was the sin lying deep within the heart of man. It's a corruption that only the death of a sinless man could cure; only Jesus. He endured it all, laying aside His mighty power for a time, being completely veiled in human flesh in order to win the war waged in the Garden of Eden.

Genesis 3:15 "He will bruise my heal, but I will crush His head!"

Hebrews 2:14 "Since therefore the children share in flesh and blood, he himself likewise partook of the same things, that through death he might destroy the one who has the power of death, that is, the devil,"

The cross of Christ destroyed Satan. Jesus dealt a single crushing blow to the Devil. The power that Satan possesses is temporary and limited. He can no longer hold captive those who trust and cling daily to that cross.

## Chapter 14
## The Cross over Fear

*"Permit me to say there is nothing in the Bible to make any man fear who puts his trust in Jesus. Nothing in the Bible, did I say? There is nothing in heaven, nothing on earth, nothing in hell, that need make you fear who trust in Jesus. "Fear not ye." The past you need not fear, it is forgiven you; the present you need not fear, it is provided for; the future also is secured by the living power of Jesus."*

—*Spurgeon*

Hebrew 2:15 "and deliver all those who through fear of death were subject to lifelong slavery."

What do you fear? Is it death? Jesus died so that through Him you would be delivered from fear?

Matthew 10:28 "And do not fear those who kill the body but cannot kill the soul. Rather fear him who can destroy both soul and body in hell."

We should fear neither devil nor man. Maybe it's not Satan you fear, but you do fear his abilities, his crafty schemes against the saints of God; his attempts to bring destruction to the Church and to your life. We have all been there. We have believed the lies about God whispered in our ears saying, "Did God really say…?" "Will he really take care of you?" "Are you really good enough for heaven?" "Your children will never learn." "You're not good enough to have any friends." But again, the cross of Christ is our weapon in this war. There is nothing more powerful to properly steer our hearts and our minds back to trusting God for all things. If the death of Christ on the cross crushed Satan, and the very power of death, then going back to that place is necessary in order for us to win our daily battles.

Let's consider the Church of Smyrna in Revelation chapter 2 for a moment. They were a persecuted church and under heavy tyrannical rule. They were told not to fear what they were about to suffer. The strength for this was a view of the cross. The Apostle John wrote a letter on behalf of Christ to this suffering and fearful church.

Revelation 2:8 "The words of the first and the last, who died and came to life."

Revelation 2:10-11 "Do not fear what you are about to suffer. Behold, the devil is about to throw some of you into prison, that you may be tested, and for ten days you will have tribulation. Be faithful unto death, and I will give you the crown of life. He who has an ear, let him hear what the Spirit says to the churches. The one who conquers will not be hurt by the second death."

It is clear that Satan involves himself in man's affairs, firing his spiritual darts in very physical ways, seeking to steal, kill and destroy. In the midst of this, John reminds the Church of the crucified and risen Christ. When we see Christ and the fullness of what He accomplished through His death and resurrection, we also find help in our trouble and strength to fight fear.

We must realize that spiritual war is always happening. The devil is relentless. When we fail to see this and begin to fight in the flesh, rather than relying on Christ's victory, it is then that we are overcome.

I mentioned earlier that the Enemy will often whisper lies in your ear. These are all answered by looking to the cross. "Will He really take care of me?" Look at the cross and see that His care is so immense that it extends from this life into eternity.

Romans 8:32 "He who did not spare his own Son but gave him up for us all, how will he not also with him graciously give us all things?"

The Devil may say, "Are you really good enough for heaven?" The doubts will enter in and depression may set in as you look to your own strength. But looking to the cross and to the Word of God, you'll find rest. The answer to this doubt is that *Jesus* is good enough for Heaven. He is the *only* one worthy. He died in our place on the cross. You can rest in His goodness and in His merit to bring you safely home. Remind the enemy and the world often that you already know you're not good enough. You should never have believed that you were in the first place. Trust Christ completely for this and His cross will comfort your doubting soul.

Romans 5:8-11 "but God shows his love for us in that while we were still sinners, Christ died for us. Since, therefore, we have now been justified by his blood, much more shall we be saved by him from the wrath of God. For if while we were enemies we were reconciled to God by the death of his Son, much more, now that we are reconciled, shall we be saved by his life. More than that, we also rejoice in God through our Lord Jesus Christ, through whom we have now received reconciliation."

What do we have through the life He gave? We have rejoicing, victory over sin, and triumph over the Enemy. That which seeks to exalt itself against these eternal truths, truths that have been sealed by the blood of Christ, will be thrown down.

2 Corinthians 10:3-6 "For though we walk in the flesh, we are not waging war according to the flesh. For the weapons of our warfare are not of the flesh but have divine

power to destroy strongholds. We destroy arguments and every lofty opinion raised against the knowledge of God, and take every thought captive to obey Christ,"

# Chapter 15
# The Greatest Satisfaction

*"God has so made man's heart that nothing can ever fill it but God himself."*

—*Spurgeon*

Psalm 73:25-26 "Whom have I in heaven but you? And there is nothing on earth that I desire besides you. My flesh and my heart may fail, but God is the strength of my heart and my portion forever."

In the context of Psalm 73, Asaph considers two lifestyles. He is noticing the world around him, full of sin, yet seeming to have no consequence for it. He sees the riches, pleasures, and prideful arrogance. Like the Psalmist, you too have looked around the world and noticed how it seems to prosper even in its rebellion. Later in this text,

Asaph, in his despair, comes to question the worth of being clean and forgiven before God. *Is it worth it, or would I be better off as the world?*

Look for a moment at all the world's wealth, and all that you could have if you turned today to a life of selfish gain. How does it compare with the riches of Christ and life in Him? Does it even compare? Are the temporary riches of this world even worth comparing with the riches found in Jesus? His riches are eternal. The world's riches will fade to nothing.

When you compare your life with a temporal world and with fallible man, your need for self-adequacy grows, and this is destructive. If your focus is upon temporal things, and worldly things that do not hold intrinsic worth, but have value granted to them, then true satisfaction is impossible. Asaph remained in this place until he entered the sanctuary of God. There, his perspective was washed clean to see the truth. There, worldly pleasures were proven worthless. The sanctuary of God brought bringing perspective to Asaph's soul, and there he could see that while all else is worthless, God alone is worthy. True satisfaction is coming in to view.

The sanctuary of that day was the temple and its primary purpose was for communion with God. Today God communes with His people in a new temple, a more intimate one, one that the Apostle Paul says is in the human heart.

2 Corinthians 6:16 "For we are the temple of the living God; as God said, "I will make my dwelling among them and walk among them, and I will be their God, and they shall be my people."

If right seeing, right perspective, value, and satisfaction are found in the presence of God, and getting to God is through Jesus Christ, then where should you go when you doubt? Where should you go to gain perspective again? You go to the cross.

Once there, I believe you will find the words of Asaph on your own lips. As He saw his life through the eyes of God He began to declare God as supreme, and in that, he found the deepest satisfaction, the kind the world knows nothing about.

"Whom have I in heaven but you? And there is nothing on earth that I desire besides you."

Does this mean there are no options besides God? There are many to tempt the human heart. The text simply means that all other options are worthless in comparison. Go ahead and seek the earth. Explore the vastness of the universe to find what can fill the deepest longings of your soul. But until you set your gaze upon the Almighty, you will never be satisfied.

"My flesh and my heart may fail, but God is the strength of my heart and my portion forever."

A right view of God is also the way to rightly view yourself. Asaph knew the weakness of His flesh, and that his heart was prone to failure. You are no different. No man ever has been. All flesh is weak and unable. The flesh of man can do nothing apart from God *but* fail him. That is its nature. Therefore, the spiritual man is not to be surprised by his failing heart and weak flesh. In this realization he must cling to the unfailing strength of God, and the unending portion which He supplies.

John 6:63 "It is the Spirit who gives life; the flesh is no help at all. The words that I have spoken to you are spirit and life."

These are the words of Christ. Strength and a sense of true belonging are found in Him. The strength found in Asaph's heart is only due to God. This truth, that God is all in all, is where you will find that your portion is full; full in Him.

## Chapter 16
## A Full Portion

> *"For me there shall be no deadly snares in life, nor horrible tempest in death. So long as I abide in this body, I shall be fed upon Your goodness, and when I shall fall asleep and shall afterwards awaken in the likeness of my Redeemer, I shall find myself in eternal possession of my God who is my All in All."*
>
> —*Spurgeon*

GOD IS AN eternal portion, the end of all need. In God there is no lack and in Him we find fullness of satisfaction. What does it mean to be truly satisfied?

At dinner time, my children would ask for seconds, thirds, and even fourths if allowed. In a world where many families survive whole days on quantities that amount to small percentages of our first helpings, we need to learn and relearn what it means to be satisfied. For our kids it becomes a lesson in self-control, but it also provides the opportunity for us to define for them, and remind ourselves of the true meaning of satisfaction.

Our bodies were built with appetite and designed to long for more. When we get something that we like, even though it fills us for a time, we still run back for more. Why is this? It's because we are not satisfied with the portion, and when it comes to material things, we never seem to be.

To be truly satisfied in something means that *it* must include *everything* you need. The Scriptures declare that this is God. He is the all loving, all knowing, all wise, deeply-satisfying, eternal God. In Him there is no lack. With Him, there is no need to go elsewhere for seconds, or thirds. With God as your portion you are filled to the utmost. The emptiness that sets in from time to time is not because of God's lack, but your own misdirection; seeking the wrong source.

You can look to Jesus for this example of what it means to desire and what it means to be full. The Son of God put on flesh for that very purpose, so that He could become your example in everything, your sympathizing High Priest who knows your very frame. He hungered and desired, and teaches us how to direct our hungers and desires towards a life of glorifying God.

John 4:30-34 "They went out of the town and were coming to him. Meanwhile the disciples were urging him, saying, 'Rabbi, eat.' But he said to them, 'I have food to eat that you do not know about.' So the disciples said to one another, 'Has anyone brought him something to eat?' Jesus said to them, 'My food is to do the will of him who sent me and to accomplish his work.'"

Jesus is showing His disciples that there is much more to life than food or physical appetite. He teaches them that when you have a portion from God, a portion that exceeds all else, your desire for the world grows dim. He said "My food." In other words, the portion He had been given was to do the will of God. What is your "food"? Do you recognize the portion which God has given you in Christ? Are you filled with Him; or are you dissatisfied because you fill yourself too often with the portions of this world?

The portion which Jesus received from the Father is the same for you and for me. Though most of us will never hang upon a cross the way He did, we still are given a portion and it is our job to run after it. We should imitate Christ in this and learn to be satisfied in the simplicity of doing and accomplishing God's work. For Jesus, this work was the cross. It was His mission. His portion in life was to be brought to the point of death for the ones He loved. In this He glorified God.

John 6:27 "Do not work for the food that perishes, but for the food that endures to eternal life, which the Son of Man will give to you. For on him God the Father has set his seal."

This text comes after the famous account of feeding the five thousand. The very same men and women, who had been filled with bread, sought him again. They hungered for more bread. They desired to be satisfied in their flesh once more. This time though, instead of multiplying more loaves and fish, He spoke of an eternal portion, a portion of Bread which would come down from Heaven to fill hungry souls.

They began to ask for a sign like the manna which Moses provided in his day. Jesus said He would provide a food that endures, one that will never perish. Could He be greater than Moses in this way? He surely was, for He *is* the eternal Bread from Heaven of which He speaks. Jesus corrected their misunderstanding. He said that only God supplies bread from Heaven. Moses was a recipient just like the children of Israel. Standing before them now was another portion from God, the Bread who came down from Heaven to give eternal life to His people. How does He give life? He did it by giving up His own on the cross. That is the ultimate portion for our lives. It is there that reconciliation, satisfaction and peace were purchased for an undeserving and hungry people.

It is no question that the cross glorified the Father. The Father sent the Son for that very purpose. When you seek to do the will of the Father as Jesus did, you too, will fulfill your greatest purpose in bringing God glory, and in that, find your deepest satisfaction.

The world seeks satisfaction in many places, and pays lofty prices to attain what it believes will satisfy, but it does so only to come up empty again. This happens when God is not at the base and the height of what you seek. If God does not fill the breadth of all you seek in this short life, then you live in vain, and you will die in your sin having worshiped the false god of self-satisfaction. I do believe it is that serious. I am very closed-minded to the exaltation of anything or anyone other than the God we see in Scripture. And you should be too. His holiness demands worship. His splendor and beauty call for praise. His majesty and perfection command respect and awe. Only the Creator, Jesus Christ can do this.

Job 38 "Then the LORD answered Job from the whirlwind: 'Who is this that questions my wisdom with such ignorant words? Brace yourself like a man, because I have some questions for you, and you must answer them. Where were you when I laid the foundations of the earth? Tell me, if you know so much. Who determined its dimensions and stretched out the surveying line?' 'What supports its foundations, and who laid its cornerstone as the morning stars sang together and all the angels shouted for joy? Who kept the sea inside its boundaries as it burst from the womb and as I clothed it with clouds and wrapped it in thick darkness? For I locked it behind barred gates, limiting its shores.' I said, 'This far and no farther will you come. Here your proud waves must stop!' 'Have you ever commanded the morning to appear and caused the dawn to rise in the east? Have you made daylight spread to the ends of the earth, to bring an end to the night's wickedness? As the light approaches, the earth takes shape like clay pressed beneath a seal; it is robed in brilliant colors. The light disturbs the wicked and stops the arm that is raised in violence.' 'Have you explored the springs from which the seas come? Have you explored their depths? Do you know where the gates of death are located? Have you seen the gates of utter gloom? Do you realize the extent of the earth? Tell me about it if you know!'"

The only proper response to a life given by God is praise to the One who is higher than all! There is no one like Him in all the earth!

This is Jesus! He was there. He has the preeminence and authority over ALL. But wait a minute. Didn't He die by the hands of evil men who overpowered Him and nailed Him to a cross? Think again. Jesus said "No man takes my life, but I lay it down of my own accord." His obedience to go to the cross and bear your sin glorified God above all else. We know this because before the foundations of the world the lamb was slain. The cross was in mind. The plan of sacrifice was in place to purchase each of God's children back from death and make them His children forever. The whole volume from Genesis to Revelation speaks of His cross. It's the center stage of God's plan throughout eternity. The apostle John was taken by the Spirit into the future glory of Heaven and there, he beheld Christ. What did He see there before the throne in Heaven? What will you see?

Revelation 5:6 "And between the throne and the four living creatures and among the elders I saw a Lamb standing, as though it had been slain"

I want to tell you, finally, that the cross of Christ is God's theme for the universe. Shouldn't it be yours as well? Consider the life you live and why you are here. Make a beeline to the cross to find love, joy, victory, cleansing, peace, true satisfaction and redemption. Acknowledge the cross often. Remember how it existed in the mind of God for all eternity as the greatest display of love and glory. Consider this. Once you've tasted the best, is there anything left to taste? Once you've seen the most beautiful, what is there left to seek? This is the cross, the highest and best of all that God desires for you. It is there that He purchased you. It is there that He proved His love for you and made you His own. At the cross is where you see Jesus, bleeding, crying and forgiving those who put Him there. Take everything you have; all your doubts and fears; all your joys and praises, and make a beeline for the cross. May your greatest desire be Jesus, the very One who made you, and you will truly lack nothing.

www.ingramcontent.com/pod-product-compliance
Lightning Source LLC
Chambersburg PA
CBHW070322100426
42743CB00011B/2526